HURRICANE CENTER

GEOFFREY PHILP

HURRICANE CENTER

PEEPAL TREE

First published in Great Britain in 1998
Peepal Tree Press
17 King's Avenue
Leeds LS6 1QS
England

ISBN 1 000715 23 6

For Don Paco, Doña Anatolia, Katia, Tania
and Francisco

give thanks to phyllis washington, my friend; meg o'brien, who helped me to envision this manuscript; francisco patiño, my idren (what more can i say?); martha mc donough, who saw my earliest poems twenty years ago and said i was a poet; erika waters and *the caribbean writer* for their enormous help over the years; phyllis mcewen and the florida humanities council, for the opportunity to lecture and really *see* the state; nancy holmes and the seaside institute for the time and space to re-think my priorities; gina cortes-suarez, josett peat, linda tixier, and jeffrey lukenbill of miami-dade community college, whose confidence gave me the freedom to explore and create; jillian daniel and the metro-dade cultural art affairs, whose financial assistance came at a crucial time; mary luft of tigertail productions, whose support of *the bicycle poets* and *new caribbean writing* allowed me to expand the performance of these poems; and finally, the florida arts council, whose generous grant enabled me to complete this manuscript.

CONTENTS

NEW YEAR POEM

(for meg)

inside the living room, christmas lights
still strung around the sides of the house,

our lives synchronised to dick clarke's evergreen
voice on the t.v., counting down the last seconds

of '95, final as a sentence that blacks out
starke's power twice a year; easterlies

topple potted palms that surround the cheap
figures of joseph and mary bowing to the plastic

child in our makeshift nativity and spill dry
earth on the lawn: the first gusts of a cold

front that has passed through miami
for as long as anyone cares to remember,

enough for some to find comfort in a bottle
or bullet: answers to the question of so many

possibilities, yet no solution to the poison
that brightens the leaves of the poinsettia

while the blue earth whirls though black space,
and el niño stirs clouds over the pacific, drowning

live oaks and melaleucas alike, husks
of senna, magnolia in the tiny rivulets that slip

through the cracks in everglades' drained crust,
filled with this new year's rain.

ELEMENTAL: A BLESSING

(for paul smith)

a line of school children,
my daughter in front, growing
up so fast away from me,
loops around the playground –
like our usual trek
up plumbago path, daisy avenue
to buttercup drive, and my sister
three years behind, struggling to keep up
after we found angela's body,
fearing the blackheart man
who snatched children away
from their parents; miami,
too, has blackheart men,
common as sinkholes that swallow
whole families in their homes,
or those gators that slither
along the side streets and canals
in our neighbourhood;
so i mutter a childhood psalm,
(only a fool has such a faith)
to protect her against the god
of this place, of storm, sand,
and sea, that the sun will not
burn the colour from her eyes,
the wind will not scar her cheeks,
the rain will not beat too hard
on her head, and watch as she
disappears into the uniformed crowd.

EASTER SONG

On the walkway between the warner
building and saunders pavilion, mt. sinai,
a boy, recorder in hand, practices, “row, row
row your boat” to bands of gold lantanas
sunning under the tinted dome
of the ruth and sidney harris garden
with its iron butterfly mounted
near the corner where my daughter sips
water from a fountain – above her head:
to my husband, the love of my life –
while the other kids play hide-and-seek
around the statue of the burning bush –
a symbol of god’s love for humanity
above our heads, so many dead, dying,
overlooking the emerald bay, battered
in the wake of cruisers ploughing
past idlers this easter sunday, on our yearly
ritual to present ourselves, the children,
to my wife’s god parents: don luis, always
nattily dressed, with so few months to live,
a paisley suit on a stick, his lungs, liver, soon
his cortex invaded by colonies of corpuscles, plotting
their own death; doña asela, always the stronger,
floral nightie, stubs of hair, gray to the root, held
bravely by pink ponytail holders, the shoals
of her mind nibbled by the sea of a further shore.
she barely recognises us, the children, so we apologise
for not visiting more often; don luis whispers
over the sand in her throat, “todos tenemos
zapatos que nos aprietan,” and as we leave
the garden, its queen palms shrubbed
by bachelor buttons, we glimpse the stone
flame behind him, for it still burns,
it still burns.

raise his carcass against the blackened sky,
this boy's hide isn't worth a damn.

wasn't he their saviour, their wondrous son of man?
stretch out his arms, let's see if he can fly.

listen to him bawl, mumbling into his beard,
"father, forgive them, they know not what they do."

give me that spear, i'll teach that crazy jew!
ram it up his ribs, into the heart, that'll quiet him for good.

where are all your brothers, your so-called disciples?
deserters, they said they'd follow you up the bloody cross!

that one who broke bread with you, he cut off my lobe,
where's he hiding now, behind some woman's robe?

man, you got only you, cut these lackeys for a loss:
forget them now, they were never your people.

MARY'S SONG

i guess, to you, i was just
another silly girl wanting to be seduced

by your words, "blessed art thou
among women," and believed you:

took him in, breast fed him through colics, bathed
him with my tears when his fevered cries startled

the goats, wrapped his legs, wrinkled like simeon's,
whose warnings i ignored as the fervour of an old man,

his pupils scarred from the visions that burned
behind his eyes, never thinking (was it your pride

or my desire?) that you'd break me in half,
betray me, to bring me closer to your love?

CONFESSION

mama, i'm sorry i didn't stop them
when they called you a whore.

i should have rained the fires of gehenna
or called bears out of the hills,

but it's just that from egypt to galilee,
dusty streets proclaim my shame;

they've been calling me joseph's jacket,
and it's been hell. i know, i know

he's not my father, but he's taught
me more about forgiveness

than all my sermons on hillsides;
an illegitimate prophet with a step-father

who forgave god for fornicating
with his betrothed, so that's why i came home

to lower my head and bless the dusty mound
where his bones, swaddled in dirt, lie.

so how can i judge this woman who will be
stoned as an adulteress, who quivers

like a stalk of wheat on the plains of sharon;
how can i condemn her for human

passion, the blind need for another's
arms to say she matters?

CENTURION

how come i never get any
famous criminals? i wanted to nail

that zealot until the crowd passed him
over for this dreadlocked jew;

this one could have been stopped in time
with his talk of the kingdom within;

everyone knows peace is more important
than just following a path where no one

(not even him) knows where it leads;
we have philosophers, gladiators in arenas,

epicurean festivals, fertility dances to venus,
and when things look bad, a senator

always sacrifices himself for public spectacle,
all for the good of the republic;

so let them keep looking in the desert
for some scrawny salvation, we've got the cure

BEDWARD'S BROTHER

i could have done that: climbed the steeple
of the highway, hurled myself down without bruising

my heel against a stone, called down
lightning, blood, and brimstone on leviathan

in whose belly i live with these other parasites
who feed on each other's flesh: the darker

the meat, the sweeter the flavour;
cried out to the heavens, and declared myself god,

switched my name to john x, john uhuru, john tafari
or whatever;

eaten only fallen fruit, breathed through muslin,
restricted my steps to four a day in each direction

to appease the elements until my flesh
became food for weeds, but for what? for these

orphans seeking miracles from a paunched
obeah man, who'd dig the gold out of my wisdom

teeth, whose only pleasure is rum & coke
in a hammock between almonds while a red

sun rises from a blue sea, and that is all?
better to climb down, move through the streets

like a vagrant angel, they'd never believe me.
they'd want to see the brother fly.

I'M DREAMING OF A WHITE SUMMER

today, i want to be white man.
stroll over to south beach with american express,
lounge at the fountainbleau, maybe i'll get a sun tan,
rent a cabana without causing the manager distress.
i think i'll take the weekend off, peck the wife, kids
and dog, (mind you not in that order) good-bye,
take communion on sunday, withdraw my funds
on monday from a garment factory in haiti.
hey, it's me against them. better them. i deserve
this, i can pile those numbers, just like boesky
i didn't get this far wearing my heart on my sleeve.
i don't give a flying (you know what) what anyone says.
it's me, and me alone in this big wide world.
i paid full tuition at u.m., i know what's going on.
everyone's got a price to be bought and sold.
today, i want to be a dead man.

MIAMI MAMBO

down biscayne boulevard where neon and money talk
about the blitzkrieg of bayside, a german tourist, white as chalk,
bus stop as his bunker, dodges six bullets meant for his head.
one inch closer and he'd have been brain dead,
two seconds later, he'd be revived as mayor of metro-dade
bellowing, "welcome to south beach! now sit back and get laid."

all around miami radios blare, "mama, que sera lo que quiere el negro?"
brother, can you spare some weed for an honest bro?

the dream, bawded in alapattah, liberty city, overtown,
crusts over fetid pavements, a scab turned rust-brown;
kids in reeboks boast t-shirts of malcolm and martin king junior
but they all want to be famous like little yummy sandifer.
and scampering crabs down at city hall
are climbing over each other's necks so they can fall
for the next kickback, the next riot to earn their pay,
for green's the only apartheid in condos over biscayne bay;
singing the old r&b, "black is beautiful", proud as crispus attucks,
but, baby, black aint worth nothing if it can't read a book.

all around miami radios blare, "mama, que sera lo que quiere el negro?"
brother, can you spare some weed for an honest bro?

a puffed-up heron scours the vacant beach
las playas de la habana are still beyond his reach.
he sees worms everywhere, pecks at newspapers on the docks
if he flaps louder, he'll be el presidente of an invading flock.
while on another bank, battling for sand atop an ancient hill
old victors stand on a balcony overlooking the citadel;
lips curled in a grin, now a snarl, for law and order,
behind them rotted corpses as they snake across the border.

all around miami radios blare, "mama, que sera lo que quiere el negro?"
brother, can you spare some weed for an honest bro?

and those imperious eagles, endangered in the glades,
get rarer every summer as they follow the tide
stealthily as carpetbaggers: this land's not worth a sack
of yucca, except, perhaps, what's that? casinos and blackjack?
and, ah, fellow termites what sound will you make
busy with your mounds at weston, arvida by the lake?

all around miami radios blare, "mama, que sera lo que quiere el negro?"
brother, can you spare some weed for an honest bro?

STORM WARNING

over the atlantic, off the gold coast,
hurricanes churn through the caribbean;
helmeted soldiers, intent as attachés, taper
their bayonets for news of looting; a swarm
of flying ants, homeless as those rambling tribes
under the i-95 that share space with pigeons,
roots in the sears tower, abandoned to swift cars
flitting through traffic lights along biscayne boulevard,
riddled with random cries, and quarrels over a rock,
yet ignored by the blue jays' flap – their wings
percussive as petro, beating towards their own nests.
storefronts, masked with paper, explode
like generators, and flashing t.v. screens urge calm,
but no one believes, switching from station to station to station,
retreating to the cellular security of gated dens,
guarded by armies of drones; electric eyes
protect a creaking boardwalk from gales coiled
around the centre, glowering over the dunes.

ODE TO RED STRIPE

bartender, give us another round of draft beer,
and turn up the volume on the tv,
for i don't think that i'm going home tonight
to that rented one-room apartment or my woman,
because me and my bredren going play
quarters, and i'm not stopping until i'm drunk.

now you shouldn't blame a man for getting drunk,
especially a man who can only afford beer.
i don't smoke crack or ganja, eat brie, or go to plays;
chips, anything that goes to my heart, i eat watching tv
with my legs propped up in the lazy boy, but my woman
doesn't like it when we're all there for monday night

football, and she's wearing the sexiest, see-through nightie,
and all i want to do is slap high-fives and get drunk.
it's a guy thing, like going out shopping is a woman
thing: she gets her kicks from k-mart sales, and me from beer.
sometimes with that qvc or home shopping on the cable tv,
she gets excited, like a kid with nintendo, the way she plays

with the remote, and if i touch it, or accidentally hit play
on the vcr, i'm going to sleep on the sofa that night.
and friday is always a big fight about who's controlling the tv,
but i always back off, i never fight her when i'm drunk.
i just go over in a corner with a six pack of beer,
and watch her shop and save, for you can't fight with a woman,

and win. drink beer instead. besides, which woman
can take the place of beer? you tired and she's out playing
the fool. nobody ever had a friend like a glass of beer.
that's why i'm not going home tonight,
for last week, every day, i've been getting drunk,
and she's been home, all alone, watching tv,

and when i get to the bed, she turn off the tv,
roll over, and pull the sheet between her legs: that's a woman
for you. i'm feeling frisky, and she says that my beer
breath not romantic. who want romance? i just want to play
under the covers with the vcr blinking through the night
and morning wash over me like a shower of beer.

tonight, the war between me and my woman goes on.
she won't play with me, so i going watch tv with my friends.
beer's never let me down or deserted me, and that's why i get drunk.

if me was you, me wudn lef de complex, sah.
yu have clean towel, an yu bed mek evry mornin.

free food, buffey runnin, brekfas, lunch an dinner –
all yu haffi do is ask, an smady come runnin.

lef yu money pan de bed, nobody nah tief it.
walk inna yu birthday suit, dis is all inclusive paid,

tourist tip worth more than wha inna yu wallet.
stay inside de room, yu got a roof over yu head

for once yu decide to leave, step thru dem gate,
is a different jamaica dat guwane judge yu tan.

smilin faces dat been trained to smile and greet
guwane tun to screwface of unemployed yout

who been eatin scraps from de buffey when yu dun.
so enjoy de trip, stay behind walls, an bade inna de sun.

(ii)
rent-a-dread

but wha me love is dis
white girl, innocent as a sanderling,

who in the states would never
put a french braid in her hair,

smoke a menthol cigarette,
brush gainst a black man,

sip a glass of wine after dinner,
or open the top of she blouse

in the hottest chicago summer,
but once she come in the island

without anybody knowing,
start smoke spliff bigger than me

head, suck down white rum
that rotten john crow belly,

sprawl out, with dreadlocks
in her hair, naked on the sand,

putting silverfish to shame,
or lock up, tighter than two squid,

with some natty rasta,
who for the foreign exchange,

must be happy with the white
wife, so when she go home,

brown as nutmeg, with tan lines
she will never show again,

she can take back the name
she never lose.

FANTASY LAND

across the everglades, billboards
with tanned coppertone babes dot paradise

paved over by asphalt along alligator alley,
free from potholes; below high tension

voltage lines, safe by developer's standards,
and canals choked by cane fields,

fast-food diners squeeze
out by roadside nude bars with dancers

old enough for medicare,
yet advertise, "girls, girls, girls!"

disney world, secure on each side,
a model for urban strategists, looms

along the interstate, where cartoon
daisies, minnies, sleeping beauties,

all wonderful and white, are welcome
under the dome of epcot

and are forever young
in a betty boop playground.

ODE TO WASHINGTON

george, when the good old boy
from davie strokes inside my garter, you'll
realise i'm a pretender. under these lights
with the bass player, his thick fingers treading
through my favourite descargas, it's easy to fool
everyone with the roll and groove of my sex:
si, marielita, sister to these hairs that are dyed
and waxed; truth is, not even my navel's real;
so he'll flop into bed, eyes afloat in a yellow
brew with a trick of strobes and smoke, believing
i'm the all american girl without a tan line,
for the tattooed biker bitch's the only natural
blonde in this dive; so when i try to sleep, drown
the last valium, remember, george, i'm trying
to dream your dream; tonight, george, as the light
leaves your face under a motel lamp, explain
to my husband in cuba why i left him.

SEPARATION

papers signed, the taxi waited
below; i would keep the dog, apartment,
mortgage; you wanted only the clothes

in your bag; streetlights burned
through the window. "you'll write, i mean,
keep in touch somehow?" the clock bartered

for another minute, ash from your
cigarette fell on the carpet, the driver shrugged,
blew the horn. i wanted to hold

you like the night we clasped
like scorpions exchange venom, resolute
as the river between my hands, but stones

in your voice's current, like turned sheets,
betray my name. the driver honked
again; this is a cold bed.

A DAY AT THE RACES

"yu bet yu life," the drawsy touter say,
dunzai tight in him fist, "that likkle mare
cyaan stan up to my stallion, the mighty saga boy!"
so i put my money where my mouth was, an stare

him down. "my girl's a thoroughbred. i feel it in me soul."
match him dollar fa dollar wid me rent money an buy the ticket.
but i wasn't staying at the roadside off course to get it
from a radio announcer who doant know filly from foal.

i lef de buway sweating like a jackass, him partner a groan,
leg lock tighter than a jockey in the stirrup,
riding the beast, from starting post to the finish line,
galloping so hard, him waist ready to pop.

race start. saga boy have blinders, a mane of black hair,
and my girl, a one year old maiden, wasn't looking
too bad herself as they turn into the shoulder,
two furlongs to go, and my girl in front, but picking

up the rear, saga boy coming on fast,
with me holding on, like love, to me battered stub.
saga boy and my girl so close, saddle start to rub,
saga boy and my girl, neck and neck, dead heat;

saga boy on top of my girl with a furlong to go;
i beggin, "lawd, mek it done," and start think instead
i shoulda bet even a dollar with my girl to show.
photo finish; the bleachers went wild. saga boy in by a head.

DANCE HALL: VERSION

you see me dying trial, gun inna the dance:
after me wake up with crosses, gingy fly
round my head, like i was deaf, crosses inna me

bed like ants crawling over me chest, inna the yard
rubbing themself gainst the tamarind, make me want
to fling this bag of bone like it worth a raas?

after light man lock off the fridge, spoil me food,
water man cut off the pipe, boss man meet me with soap
in me beard, evening find me clothes in a pothole

of mosquito, landlord padlock the door, change
the key, and all me come the dance is to sip some man-
ish water, rent-a-tile, clean the cobweb from the corner

of me brain while i hole a dawta, and slip
me hand over her warm breast with the sweet
smell of herb climbing up her skirt, and the one

thing on me mind is that the boots don't burst,
and sing in time with gregory isaacs, the cool
ruler on the turntable, yes, yes, yes.

REEL FROM PORT-AU-PRINCE

the city, necklaced with smoke,
breathes mist from corrugated zinc;

the sun burns like napalm
through rust-red clouds, and rags

like men, dangle in the wind
orphaned by a vendor's cart;

my sister scales fish amidst shrapnel
and fire-bombed hotels; flesh

yields casually to her touch;
she slices the heart like light,

and washes blood from the sidewalk
while children swing from turrets:

their taut bodies punctuate hopscotch
rhymes scrawled on sides of ford pickups

parading farm queens under papier-mache
mushrooms, for we still manage a carnival air

and dance with guede: this woman is not my wife,
i am not her husband, yet she hugs my green fatigue

like eyes that burn holes in the fence:
"who else has disappeared? who else

has screamed in the night, never to be
heard? who's next?" questions scorch

like the fahd's cigarette against my nape,
meaningless as the stars across his chest.

in that still frame, ma boyer, bandaged
by her manbo scarf, offers her palms,

crisscrossed like wires from the rafters,
for there is no more bread, no more light.

I HAD TO LEAVE A LITTLE GIRL...

soon you, too, would become
ordinary. eyes that once brightened dawn,

dull to formica gray, breasts, pert naseberries,
droop into their speckled skin;

those four hour phonecalls about vacations
in mo bay, turn to talk of bills, bills,

bills, and children, sepia-cheeked cherubim,
mutate to monsters that eat

eat, eat and i haunt each room
with a singular thought, turn off

the light, turn off the light. yet there are certain
nights when our cat scales the fence

in a single motion, when i still believe i own
this house, this car, this life, and a sock

dangles aimlessly from the avocado, i forget
the folded sheets, the prim order of your bed.

8 O'CLOCK ROAD BLOCK
OR
PRELUDE TO A RIOT

(to tony mcneill)

today
traffic was held up by a black man
who'd hiked atop the highway railing, and stayed up there
although his mother, wife, and girlfriend
pleaded with him to come down
until a cop said enough
was enough, and secured by ropes, strung
without the blackman's knowledge,
grabbed at the blakman's shirt,
which he let go
without a fight, then his pants, everything,
till he stripped down to complete blkness
and let go
again
his body whirring through the dry air, like an electron freed
of its orbit,
sent radical isotopes
screaming from their inert base;
the city blkd out.

SCREENPLAY FOR A RIOT

flashback to a high-speed chase,
cars swerving through the city

of angels when only faggots
and homeboys come out to cruise

the strip. close up:
two bulging eyes and gold rimmed

teeth emerge behind a steering
wheel dwarfed by hands, scarred

by tufts of hair; the velvet lined
upholstery stewed in sweat, malt

liquor, littered with food
stamps, subpoenas for child support

and pictures of his wife and girlfriends;
then a voice-over: "my god, he's going

to kill us," and a father, a son, a faithful
husband unsheathe their batons, bathed

in the seraphic blue light of squad cars,
swarm helter-skelter over a slouched

body, crumpled like a fist of kleenex.
cut to the present. wide angle:

fire catapults ash into the scorched air. freeze
frame: shoot the next block.

I MAN

(for mervyn morris)

i am the man yu tun way from the door.
i am the man who face white wid yu spit,

i am the man who clean the toilet.
i am the man who live off quattie salt, quattie flour.

i am the man, screw face sharp, red as mongoose,
i am the man the asphalt paint black.

i am the man yu pass at the stoplight, lexus-quick.
i am the man wid me empty han stretch ova de fence.

i am the man yu stone, not wort yu bret,
i am the man yu cut yu eye an pass, a black blood clot.

i am the man who eat under the corner of yu house.
i am the man who live wid macca, scorpion, crab louse.

i am the man who sleep in the cradle of the banyan,
i am the man yu wudn call yu bredren.

MIDSUMMER, RAIN

rain sputters
through thin reeds,

a skirt of green nettles
blue mountain's waist, girlish

as the tributaries that scrawl
their names into towns,

past the writhing cane smoke,
mists that breathe over the hair

of cassava, yellow yams; arawak,
african villages under mud,

veins of bauxite: syllables
seep through rock and time.

NAGGO HEAD

past almonds' shade
mangroves

beside naggo head's
skull

beyond palisade swamp
hum

syllables into silent
fragments

STORM SURGE

beyond the face of mt. airy,
terraced by strict rows of corn,
surrounded by waves of barbed wire,
hemming the corners of this town,
sharper than any parson's tongue,
limestone plunges into the spray
that shatters coral gardens,
in the seconds lovers call eternity,
without fear of being broken
into palisade, cove, lagoon,
in the surge that covers and returns.

LAMENTATIONS

evry year anada fren kick off the planet:
fisher get stab by a watchman in a perfect bed,

robby from asthma, bone chillin night sweat,
angela scream paint maryland shoulder red;

lef the baptist to dey prayers, misery eatin san,
wash way in a sea cross wid tek-life current,

fa de holy sistas hosannas is nothin but win',
fannin green-eye gingy fly over me foot.

lawd, i jus scrapin by wid me belly to eart;
so low, enough scale cyaan cover me;

blind law, like a woman smile, poison each bret,
an when i clear me eye from the yellow pus

pack inna de corner, all me can see
is a dirt red country road cover wid dus.

RED LIGHT

just before –
windows rolled down to escape

mildew and bleach rising off
the back seat, a careless day

as you fumble through the mail,
envelopes with stamps of exotic

fruit, letters from lovers ten
years ago that begin, "i don't know

how to say this," or plainer
truths from the blood bank, termites

eating through the floorboards,
the rash that won't go away, spots

on the lips of the hibiscus, blooms
in your lungs on x-rays, a change

in your body's conversation
with itself – a man calls your name

and summons half your life to court,
the light turns green.

BELLE GLADE

doan hole me han, bribe me with eye water,
all day you kotch down by the stoplight
like a rusty dog around the milk crate,
so lazy, matta caulk yu mouth corner.

busha, i will work till me back ready to burs,
but why yu haffi bruk me han an foot firs?

get off you side, ants in the cane field wake up
before you, take care of them own, clean out
they nest, an you stew in rooster shit,
you eye, rolling back and forth, blinking without sleep.

busha, i will work till me back ready to burs,
but why yu haffi bruk me han an foot firs?

every day i kiss arse to live, my sweat too dear;
why i must give, for you to spend it on weed,
then sprawl out like a periwinkle on the road side,
when i can barely see, and you live without fear?

busha, i will work till me back ready to burs,
but why yu haffi bruk me han an foot firs?

SEASIDE, FLORIDA

somewhere between cafe spiaggia, bud
and alley's seductive heat, the old fear

like cold creeping into my fingers: white
light, conversion by nightsticks to a vision

of heaven, as i wheeled through the town,
a dark pelican over the houses where music

and laughter remained trapped behind unspoken
commandments, down a powdery dune that resisted

their red brick salvation and trickled off
the grid, leaving grinning posters of the elect,

news racks crowded with stories of pestilence,
war, rumours of war, before the evening fog

erased the post office: old glory limping
down the flag pole near the meeting hall, preserved

in its idea of democracy, still awed that venus
could shine clear across the gulf, strewn

with sargasso, shells broken by the water's edge,
man-o-wars, their arms severed by propellers,

when i stood, there and now, on opposite shores,
light peeping on the huiros in frayed hammocks,

asking the same question to a different sky,
then back through the lobby with my friend, her eyes

rolled upward to a galaxy of fluorescent bulbs
wondering how it would end: in a flash or a cold

whisper in a white hotel, babbling the lie
that everything was for the best when i already

knew the worst, with so many islands between us
and me still searching for my name.

ALLIGATOR ALLEY

i'm with you, brother, tanning
your thick leather, coarsened by years

of drought, beside the caloosahatchee
that empties names, outlived by america's

hunger for gold, sugar, youth, into the gulf
where you lurk, for something careless,

an innocent doe, or some aimless cane-cutter,
to stir the water and eyes will pop out of the murky

swamp, jaws crunch bones, then barely move,
secure on your all engorging stomach,

away from the allosaurus crowded
heartland, in your knowledge that victor

or victim is a matter of who has survived,
for while other dinosaurs fossilize into oil,

splattered across the highway, you lumber beside
the stiff palmettos, waiting for the next aeon to pass.

TULUM

in the caves of tulum
with the other tourists,
and my sister-in-law, a transplanted
colombian, via new york, miami, caracas,
my eyes shift in darkness;
our guide from xumal, a local,
shrieks, "xosh, xosh," at the young
beggars gathered at the mouth
of the caves like gregarious bats,
in a tongue that brochures
explain has seeped into the vines
under the padded soles of the tizon
surrounding chichen itza, home of chac
mol, whose pyramids pierce the rain
clouds; our guide points along the wall
at the studded relief of random
shadows and tries to understand
how we cannot see
the virgin of guadalupe
the head of the jaguar
the flower in the stone
the face of god?

AFTERMATH

the house finally boarded up
we decided to go inside

to seek shelter and guard
what was left till the torrent stopped;

the radio hummed with the coleman's torch
and we waited for the gusts to tear,

batter to pulp, all that we'd left unsecure:
oranges that were out of reach,

mangoes that rotted in the grass;
the storm slammed, uprooted pine.

after the eye passed, tangled lines
slithered through the broken glass.

MANGROVE

where all the idren who used to crowd
i heel, like janga, running down the coast?
one sun, one father to the red, black, and white,
for it dread living out the freshness inside

where all the idren who used to hail i?
dem fall inna the sea so crab can build
a mansion of bone baited with blood,
gather them in scandal bags from the gully

where all the idren who used to love i?
springing from sand that full of poison,
i grow in the killing bed of creation;
out here, i house, alone, is sanctuary

NOT ANOTHER AIDS POEM

(for hernando)

when did the tissues,
the invisible barrier between cells,
break and send nuclei,
intent on their own destruction,
alerting an armada of antibodies
in your body's mutiny against itself?

i ask because it's
the only question that i can understand,
with which i can console myself
while i mutter
a new alphabet of ddc, azt, ddi...
and you become a mottled ghost
in a gown, transparent as
your skin, a part of the bed,
a network of tubes,
roots i cling to

that connect this life to the next

THE GARDEN

"peel head john crow siddung a tree top
eat off the blossom" – jamaican folk song

this garden i keep
with its bloom of african violets

against my skin,
overrun with fire ants, chinch bugs, aphids –

parasites too numerous for a single cure –
that burrow into the flesh of the fruit,

snap green tendrils on the vine and leave
rhododendrons swollen with tumors,

malignant as melanoma,
cucumbers drawn to a sack

of rotting seeds, blemishes
whiten the tongue of the anthurium,

tomatoes with nightly sweats
shiver under a cover of leaves.

the dry dog coughs at the wooden trellis,
mounted by brown veins of wild yams

sprayed with red-vialled pesticides,
more corrosive than curative,

that stiffen snails in their slime,
quails branches to the root,

but for the fragrant herb that awakens
the dasheen's desire for dew, forestalls

the harvest of night blooming cereus
flowering in the corner of the yard.

LA ROSA BLANCA

cruising along la septima, ybor city
across don quijote's red bricks
baked in tobacco, shotgun houses reduced

to verbena by the lure of progress, jose marti,
under the medal of paulina pedroso
whose husband, fed, housed, and guarded

their freedom fighter from assassins
of the cuban dream, beckons
to the pensioners from broken co-ops,

disavowed from medicare, the green leaves
of food stamps; above the white roses, divided
by splintered gardens, shaped like the provinces

of his island, (oriente, still neglected, bordered
by oyster plants, scraggly as fidel's beard,
that push tender swords through clumps of clay),

and to the homeless beside the stop signs,
they are watching us, ricardo;
watching us from the underbelly of the i-4,

behind chain link fences and gated entrances,
waiting for the harvest of thorns
from the acid crust of this, our city.

HALLOWEEN

in the duppy stories i tell my children
about the great house in big woods,

with its cedar and guinep trees whose limbs
twisted themselves through the mango grove,

their heads barely visible from cane fields
that unfurl green needles from burnt

rattoons, feather-filled lairs of mongoose,
and rolling calves behind doors

where an old man, his hands supple
as the thin strip of leather, a present

from a lodge brother he hid with other
secrets under his pillow after he dressed

his children for church on sundays,
though he never went, despite their plea's,

screams woven into fable. Yet the neighbours
swear he never drank, never smoked – never

– until the dark lessons spilled into the
streets and haunt these simple tales.

SNAPSHOT

a face stares at me from a photograph
over my bed, "do or die, semper fi,

love, oscar. u.s. marine corp, sniper."
and i think of panama when my grand-uncle

left jamaica to work the canal; cousins
who uttered "viva la patria," at every toast

of rum in cuba where my grandfather
lived until the house in struie was ready;

the silence of grand-aunts who never spoke
a word of english; of haiti where our friend, felix

and his father, and his father's father
fought against the marines, and today a grand

nephew of his throws rocks at the blancs.
my sister sleeps soundly tonight;

the republic's safe and defended,
for her son has become a real american.

FAMILY PORTRAIT

in the adjoining room
my father, pen in hand, separates

digits precisely, "one run down
the column"; no wonder he's in such

demand, still proud he doesn't use
a calculator, nothing but his mind

to balance each loss; the figures squat
on the lines, each in its own joy

of limited infinity; i try to memorise
lines from ecclesiastes about vanity

that my mother makes me learn
from the cadence of her voice –

though she can never remember
chapter or verse, mere numbers

that to him were not the thick furniture
of our living room – the implacable sofas,

robust armchairs that blocked the mouth
of his den – but were lovers, arranged in rows

neat as a telephone book, assigned their proper
place, in the sure strokes of his signature.

A LION IN WINTER

"inna the copse, you can lose yu life," beeline
said, "it have jack fruit, but macca and bush
will cut yu, water yu eye, burn up yu flesh
like the last breath of a kitchen

bitch, mek yu pray to god yu wasn' born,
and if yu crawl inna wild yam or cow itch,
and it get dung inna yu cratches,
might as was well yu get a gun;

an some part of them bushy hill
have hole start out small as yu han,
will swallow yu up like a cistern,
and if yu slip pon a wis and fall

dere's manhole deeper than wha yu read bout.
"so why," i ask him, "yu always a go cross
before morning rub sleep out it eye, if it so dangerous?"
and he said, "yu know anything else in life so sweet?"

ROOTS

eh yu,
yu likkle red kin buway
ah talkin to yu,
yu dat doan know nothin;
i rememba when yu used to
eat korn flakes fa brekfas,
chicken bres fa lunch,
steak fa suppa; fa me:
bush tea fa brekfas
pipe water fa lunch
red herring an stale bread,
if me was lucky, fa supper;
an den nat even a pilla,
de only comfort was kaya
mattress me share wid me bredda
mi sista, mi cousin (later dem say was
mi sista), an mi sista half-sista
(later dem say was mi niece);
yu dat neva know how it feel
when de chinee woman a de grocery store
draw way har han like me have disease –
yu look chinee too
fa yu look like yu mada
neva know wha side a de bed
she an yu was guwane fall;
and my own mada, out before
first light, not back until the night breeze
lay down pon de grass, har two han
too tired fe even liff de spoon to har mout,
much less fe hole me face;
yu dat neva know
how it feel wen smady pint
an sey, "look, das yu fada,
pants seam sharp like gillette,

shu't white like dry spit,
black patent leather shoes stomping
pon the cricket oval";
yu dat neva know
granny fiah stick me tink wud neva
go out, antie nerve tea dat stink up
me nose hole like de nasty claat
she put pon ar foot fa sugar;
yu doan know dese tings
yu jus stan up dey
an waan pass off yuself
as a real jamaican.

ONE SONG

when dis ya bass-line drop
is like *rebel music* bus inna mi brain:

dew fall, leaf curl, riddim dat will neva stop;
when dis ya bass line drop,

brother bob wails, *hey, mr. cop*:
shistem buckle when word-sound reign;

when dis ya bass-line drop,
is like *rebel music* bus inna mi brain.

TIGER, TIGER

when the tigers entered her body, they started
with her stomach that had flared ever since

she decided to keep the first child and drowned
the fire with the bush that grew behind her kitchen;

under the shade of eucalyptus, the tigers toyed
with her spleen, the spongy fluff on their whiskers,

her gall bladder, already shredded from years
of waiting for headlights to swing around the driveway,

for him to tumble into bed, between her breasts, smelling
of rapture or some other perfume he said they could never

afford; and as the doctors clicked their pens, nudged
interns into the hallway, her body hidden behind charts

and daily reports, the tigers savoured her liver, licked
their paws clean of the veins swollen with bile,

and while the nurses checked i.v drips, changed
bed pans, she could hear them romping

through her body, tearing the last wisps of hair
from her scalp, feel their breath against her cheeks;

and facing the orange brightness that barred her door,
their yellow eyes as they clawed her lungs, her voice

becoming hoarse as their snarls, her tongue as bloody,
answered with her own terrible roar.

MIAMI LOVESONG: A DREAM

(to joy harjo)

last night
a migraine – a pebble
rubbing against my cerebellum –

so fierce all softness hurt,
numbed me to sleep
on the sofa of the former tenants,

rosie and hy tannenbaum,
who, after temple, sat near the stoops
of the apartment complex

as the final stages of alzheimer's
toyed with the synapses of rosie's
brain: she would forget her name,

who he was; when she died, he followed
a week later; yet in my dream, a bear,
big as god, grappled with a man,

an indian, (forgive the lapse
of a west indian) like those in ten
o' clock matinees when i wore

white t-shirts, blue jeans, black shoes,
standing in line at premier for the latest
western slaughter and loved it,

living the american dream in jamaica;
and the voice of the old wrinkled poet,
for whom my "breed aint metaphysical",

said, "that man was not a dead
sound in an alley of time, he was a... "
(as with all true revelation the text

is unintelligible here) and as i turned
in the dream, the pebble rolled
from my hand in the doorway

where rosie one saturday evening
whispered in hy's ear a joke
he had told her fifty years earlier

on their wedding night,
and rosie, still blushing,
laughed like a virgin bride.

AFTER THE DIVORCE

(for thom)

outside the mandarin restaurant
with its familiar statue of gautama destined

to be toppled by a yellow caterpillar dozing
beside the amber flicker of bob's barricades, a helicopter,

its dull moon reflected off the bay's oil-
slick skin, peered through the mangrove

beds for illegals while other husbands marched
down the marina's aisle of blue tarpaulins, taut

as the masts of catamarans and flags along the docks
swore allegiance to the wind; the buddha,

in his stone nirvana, amidst a swirl of sand flies, hooded
against mosquitoes from dredged canals, sat serenely

as the yellow claw of the bulldozer chewed his golden
cranium, sent fissures across his chest, down chakras

of his spine to the flower of the pubis, perched
atop a rock turtle, at least three hundred years old,

its head bulged between his parted thighs;
with his left hand, his right razed from his lap,

signified, "fear not," as the yellow claw dipped
into his groin again.

POSTSCRIPT

another year grown between us
wrought with bitter crossings,
chaos; tumbled sheets yield their bated

questions to the cheap longing of my hands
to wrest meaning from the stammering blinds,
desperate notes left unanswered;

somewhere a jet prowls the air,
like the heart seeks metaphor
to still the mind's wakened rage,

whose logic, like the scream of turbines,
races toward nothing, sears the skyline,
trembles across the torn page.

MASQUERADE

(*to osmond watson*)

behind horsehead, pitchfork, masque,
the faces danced;

the canvas stared back,
but it did not show the boy, sardines, red herring

on his breath, running for common entrance
only to fall,
                    to end

the best three card man in the pigeon gang,

nor did it show the girls whose laughter
ended at thirteen in the back room
of the all-age secondary school

beverly, rita, and what was her name?

the one you were really in love with
or so you said

it wouldn't last
she lived below torrington bridge
where no love could cross

or mask this frenzy

from the edge of the wilderness,
under the sky's wintry glare, goats
bleat at dried streams, thin blades
sliver the ewes' tongues, camels
cough in the dust – have we gone
too far, our faith too much
like madness? for we alone are sure
of what we've seen; our sons totter
from sleepless nights; the sand
tears their eyes, our daughters'
hands, callused from pounding
corn against stones; and barely
holding our robes, we lower
our heads against the wind
that tatters whatever was left
of our pride. yet our reward
lay on the cold straw, warmed
by our bodies, so close to god:
helpless, naked, tired, cranky, one
of us, as we peered through holes
in the thatched roof, and delighted
in the dance of that star.

CHRISTMAS POEM
(for phyllis washington)

the cool december breeze
wanders through the town,

aimless as shooting stars
over a pasture where a heifer

breaks the glass of a pond
and splashes toward a clear

opening, for even the goats
have come down off the stony

hillside to rest by the roots
of the allamanda, it's time;

time to wash away
the smoke of the year's turmoil,

to put aside profits, gains, losses...
the familiar ache that brings

tears in the bathroom mirror, it's
time; time to listen to the wind's

chorus of the children's carols,
time to untie the knots in the old

men's arms, loosen the cords
around the old women's hips, crown

with poinsettias the young girls' hair,
garland the young men's shoulders, its time;

time to smooth the lines,
dampen the fires in the wrists, knees, elbows...

pour the balm of aloe over the new
skin that we are becoming

with every flicker of a second,
or a candle reflected in the faces

of those here, gone, and to come,
whose only promise is joy.

todos tenemos zapatos que nos aprietan: we all have shoes that squeeze us (p.11).

joseph's jacket: a jacket is an illegitimate child (p.14).

Bedward: a jamaican preacher who was discredited when he claimed he could fly (p.16).

mama, que sera lo quiere el negro: (pop song heard throughout miami and the caribbean) mama, what does the black man want? (p.18).

dunzai: a rastafarian term for money (p.28).

rent-a-tile: dancing so close to your partner you barely move; you've rented the tile. (p.29)

boots: condom (p.29).

fahd: haitian military officer (p.30)

huiros: mexican peasants (p.42).

Tulum: Tulum, Mexico (p.45).

scandal bags: jamaican term for plastic shopping bags (p.47).

duppy: ghost (p.52).

rolling calves: phantasm (p.52).

viva la patria: long live the homeland (p.53).

macca: thorn (p.55).

kitchen bitch: a lamp (p.47).

cow itch: poisonous shrub (p.55).

kin: skin; kin (p.56).

kaya: fibrous material used to make mattresses; marijuana (p.56).

smady: someone (p.56).

shistem: a rastafarian term for babylon system (p.58).

the old wrinkled poet: american poet laureate, robert penn warren (p.60).

ABOUT THE AUTHOR

Geoffrey Philp, author of *Exodus and Other Poems, Florida Bound* and the collection of short stories, *Uncle Obadiah and the Alien*, is the recipient of many awards for his work, including an Individual Artist Fellowship from the Florida Arts Council, James Michener fellowships at the University of Miami, and has been an artist-in-residence at the Seaside Institute. "The River", which appears in *Uncle Obadiah and the Alien*, won the Canute Brodhurst Prize from *The Caribbean Writer*.

He was born in Kingston, Jamaica, educated at Jamaica College and graduated from the University of Miami. He now lives in Miami, Florida with his wife, Nadia, and their three children, Anna, Christina, and Andrew.

Also By Geoffrey Philp

FLORIDA BOUND

For those who believe that the Caribbean starts at Miami, Geoffrey Philp's *Florida Bound* firmly establishes this quirk of geography. In the journey of these poems, leaving Jamaica and arriving in Miami, Philp meets the new blueness of "Florida waters", the traffic, the Interstate, with his heritage of lyric language. His poems are as vibrant and diverse as Miami where "each street crackles with dialects/ variegated as the garish crotons". Miami, albeit citified, becomes just one more island with all that is good, bad, and potentially violent beset by the same sea, same hurricanes, and "mangroves lashed sapless by the wind".

Philp's poems wander through bedrooms and along the waterfronts of that perceptive land accessible only to poets, only to those who can pull the day through dawn fog to the delicate "breath of extinguished candles".

Philp weaves dialect and landscape into his lines with subtle authority. It is easy to get caught up in the content and miss the grace of his technique.

"Florida Bound", the long title poem, ends the book almost as a letter home to Jamaica "where the land is a cracked gourd, a testament broken", the poet's apology for chosing exile over the deep geography of his birth; a poet tired of rulers "who teach only the whip and the rope./ ...Tired of dreams. New Jerusalems".

Carrol B. Fleming
The Caribbean Writer

64 pages £5.95 ISBN 0-948833-82-3 1995

UNCLE OBADIAH AND THE ALIEN

"If Dickens were reincarnated as a Jamaican Rastaman, he would write stories as hilarious and humane as these. Uncle Obadiah and the other stories collected here announce Geoffrey Philp as a direct descendent of Bob Marley: poet, philosophizer, spokes-person for our next new world."

Robert Antoni, author of *Blessed is the Fruit* and *Divina Trace*,
Winner of the 1992 Commonwealth Writers Prize.

Geoffrey Philp is a literary shaman, an enchanter, a weaver of spells that reveal unexpected and marvelous things about life, that carry the news of island culture to the mainland. From the first word of the first story in this comic and touching collection, Philp lifts me out of my world and drops me into the world of his charming, beleaguered and compelling characters. Uncle Obadiah and the Alien is one of those rare treasures, a book you can't put down and won't ever forget.

John Dufresne, author of *Louisiana Power & Light*

Geoffrey Philp's writing combines a poetic sensibility with finely honed narrative skills that draw on a multitude of resources: literary and oral traditions, rasta and ragamuffin flavours, science fiction and Jamaican tall tales. Philp blends them all with humour, wisdom and craft.

Norval Edwards

Pages 160, ISBN 1-900715-01-5 £5.99
1997

Peepal Tree Press publishes a wide selection of outstanding fiction, poetry, drama, history and literary criticism with a focus on the Caribbean, Africa, the South Asian diaspora and Black life in Britain. Peepal Tree is now the largest independent publisher of Caribbean writing in the world. All our books are high quality original paperbacks designed to stand the test of time and repeated readings.

All Peepal Tree books should be available through your local bookseller, though you are most welcome to place orders direct with us. When ordering a book direct from us, simply tell us the title, author, quantity and the address to which the book should be mailed. Please enclose a cheque or money order for the cover price of the book, plus 75p towards postage and packing.

Peepal Tree produces a yearly catalogue which gives current prices in sterling, US and Canadian dollars and full details of all our books. Write, phone or fax for your free copy.

You can contact Peepal Tree direct at:

17 King's Avenue
Leeds LS6 1QS
United Kingdom

tel: 44 (0)113 245 1703
fax: 44 (0)113 246 8368
e-mail hannah@peepal.demon.co.uk